BITER

BITER

Claudia Jardine

AUCKLAND
UNIVERSITY
PRESS

First published, 2023
Auckland University Press
University of Auckland
Private Bag 92019
Auckland 1142
New Zealand
www.aucklanduniversitypress.co.nz

© Claudia Jardine, 2023

ISBN 978 1 7767 1101 7

Published with the assistance of Creative New Zealand

ARTS COUNCIL OF NEW ZEALAND TOI AOTEAROA

A catalogue record for this book is available from the National Library
of New Zealand

Cover design by Philip Kelly
Internal design by Carolyn Lewis

Cover image: *Laocoön and His Sons*, marble, copy after a Hellenistic
original from c. 200 BC. Found in the Baths of Trajan, 1506.
Photo: Marie-Lan Nguyen, 2009.

This book was printed on FSC® certified paper

Printed in China by Everbest Printing Investment Ltd

for Nathaniel

Contents

ille mi par esse deo videtur

Preface

Several of the following poems are translations of epigrams recorded in the *Palatine Anthology*. An epigram is a short, concise poem with a witty turn of thought towards the end. I have translated these poems from Greek to English, and have taken some creative liberties. Readers don't need an education in the classical studies of Ancient Greece or Rome to understand these poems. The *Palatine Anthology*, it is commonly believed, was compiled in the tenth century by the Byzantine schoolmaster Constantinus Cephalas. Cephalas's compilation was likely based on even older anthologies. The epigrams in the *Palatine Anthology* are attributed to authors who lived and wrote between the seventh century BCE and the seventh century CE. The Greek language is one of the few things these authors had in common with one another.

Ode to Mons Pubis

fatty tissue, edifice of overtures
joints, ligaments, bones, cartilage
dark turns to stars when I think about
the buttress of pubic symphysis
yes! paths of faery lights, yes! brambly wads
yes! tracks of calligraphic gastropods
yes! tender grasses, yes! boxed beds
clippings from a crooner's greenhouse
topiary of the descent
one sight of the treeline and brain tells blood to bouse
erogenous zone! bumper bar!
tendons, abdominals, I know what you are!
hair-covered fat pad, fine hill for roly-polies
the best views, as we know, should be taken in slowly
but not too slowly! Byron did say that
'high mountains are a feeling,'
and this mountain, though not high, feels like
a chalet, a chassis and a beacon
oh shady stoa! sloping lawn!
diving board of channel crossings!
the panache and talent of your form
absorbs all of my worries
your body, my body, round and around
the belt of Adonis ♥ the Venusian mound
and all my moth-heart dashboard ablaze—
interrupt my Byron – ready the belays!

1

Young Hearts

Palatine Anthology V.1 — Constantinus Cephalas

young hearts
I offer hot wisdom in your temples

Love
I will show
is supreme in my stories

and Love, young hearts,
has set alight your beacons.

Rural Activities

which one was my favourite?

there was kickback from the rifle aimed at cans of spaghetti
which set my last good ear reluctantly ringing
but organs grumbled on, oblivious,
    dedicated to their business

then, a bowstring chipped along a forearm, the obvious
smarting blush of focus lost – that's all – just a rash
to impress upon oneself the importance of accuracy

how about the satisfaction of bowling straight
and spinning, after three wides?
even the llamas seemed to sense that

otherwise, catching the hawk
making hot circles in the haze
before braking hard in the macrocarpa

the host will copy her later and almost clip a concrete wall
prompting a brief vision of a herniated ute
    smoking in the darkness
but we keep to our seats and let him turn up his dust

no, hey, I know

the sheep started to seem familiar
pumping panic, split up, sorted, all of us
watching the same pink pair of shorts
thinking the shade had lost its cool and comfort

wondering how high one would jump
and if the gate could be cleared

One God

Palatine Anthology V.51 — Anonymous

I fell in love
I kissed
gains made
it all happened
I am desired

but I?
and you?
and how?
one god alone knows

Is It Hard to Follow Your Heart When You Have Three?

on the story of the giant octopus from Aelian's *De Natura Animalium* XIII.6

is it hard to follow your heart when you have three?

one for circulation
two for breathing

I am the stone jar of pickled fish
you are the giant octopus

I wait in the dark for you
you crawl up the sewer for me

we cast our votes
two are for breathing

Slap-assed

Palatine Anthology V.55 — Dioscorides

she was bedfast, unfurled, slap-assed,
and in her verdant joinery I was Styxed
astride me with feet flanks thighs superlative
she accomplished – no breaks – the cross-country of Venus
eyelids heavy, breathing heavy,
parting wet wet leaves heavy,
there she writhed, trembled, flushed
until we clipped cups, tipped out libations together
and, deliquesced, she poured forth her limbs

When We Were Courting

I sent you a picture of Canova's Theseus
and your reply was: 'woah . . . balls deep'

hard
agree

with its bovine head rolled back
arms slack
coils of rope between those tender human parts
and the ruts in the labyrinth's floor
with Prince Forgetful affixed
how could the Minotaur not be groaning?
how could those marble teeth not be parting
    in praise low and effusive? how?
how could that hand on that thigh
that saucy leg, that tilt
suggest 'the triumph of reason over irrationality'

more like 'the rump of treason topping a zoomorphic calamity'
O, Theseus! every day
you sit astride the Minotaur in the V&A
grinding your enemy's method of oppression
into the example of submissive relaxation

when we were courting
you received horny art at eight-thirty in the morning
because I wanted to say,

'look at these two
having a nice time,'
because I wanted to say,
'I need some myths rewritten
again,'
because
I wanted to say,
'when are you coming over?'

Oath

Palatine Anthology V.141 — Meleager

more than the lyre of Apollo
I wish to hear you whisper in my ear

. . . oath

Just a Thought

I depend on food fortified
with the B_{12} vitamin
to operate at premium red blood cell production
B_{12} occurs in eggs, milk
and other expulsions
I've read about nutrition
I'm a good vegetarian
and good vegetarians
scorn no alternate protein
(just a thought I have
while going down on my boyfriend)

My Iron Cervix

Whilst muttering, 'All for my sexual prime,'
I lay on the bed and tried not to faint.
The doctor was having a hard time
so the nurse held my arm, a pre-emptive restraint.

I lay on the bed and tried not to faint,
fought the urge to give doctor a kick.
Nurse held my arm, a pre-emptive restraint,
frowned as my pulse and consciousness slipped.

Fought the urge to give doctor a kick,
but the little bit of plastic wouldn't go in!
Frowning, as my pulse and consciousness slipped,
she stopped, and said, 'Your cervix is iron!'

The little bit of plastic wouldn't go in,
and the doctor was having a hard time
so she stopped, and said, 'Your cervix is iron!'
All the more for my sexual prime!

Biter

Palatine Anthology V.244 — Paulus Silentiarius

Galatea kisses loudly and long
Demo kisses softly soft
and Doris is a biter

whose excite most?
the ears are not permitted to put kisses on trial
but I've had a taste of all three – I will cast my vote!

heart, don't be baffled, you know
the soft kisses of Demo!
and you know the running honey of her mouth
sweet caramelisation!
stick to that! take no bribe!
carry to her the crown!

and if anyone delights in the other styles of kissing
indeed
no one try to convert me

Good Love

Palatine Anthology V.245 — Macedonius the Consul

you giggle
you act like a horse trying to officiate a wedding
you nod to me wordlessly
you do all you can to titillate at random

yet I swore an oath
three times I cast my vote:
never to look with kind eyes on the stones of your heart

practise kissing on your own
lick your lips without reason
pout naked
entwined with no one

I go another way
there are other, better companions
in good Love's occupation

Disturbing Suburban Magic Trick

Cilla ate six Quality Baker raspberry buns

she squirmed
belly swollen like a blimp

begin! disturbing suburban magic trick

with pink icing intact
she threw up all six

afternoon tea was ruined once again
all eyes on Dad
too proud to own a dog smaller than a footrest
besotted with our black Lab

he mumbled something about
his Great Uncle Len
and a black dog who could play cricket

a well-trained dog called Peter
who fetched, fielded and ran batters out
came when called
and put the ball down

and I thought, yeah
Great Uncle Len
Len who went up Chunuk Bair
dug shallow trenches between dead men
while his senior officers were playing cards back at camp
saw Malone split to shreds

Len would have had a well-trained dog
a friend to dig the strawberry patch in Katikati with

not like our Cilla, the overeager leg slip
who looks at us like she looks at a bin

Tiny Mammal Dream

after Fleur Adcock's 'The Pangolin'

All of my teeth are secure in my mouth,
I am wearing my clothes, and no one is dead,
and I am dressed for the occasion,
and I am not having sex somewhere I shouldn't,
and no silhouette stands backlit in my doorway.
No, it is the tiny mammal dream again,
and I am rushing about the room/paddock/party,
trying to keep something small and fast-breathing safe,
and I know the mouse/rabbit/guinea pig
will hurt itself or die unless I catch it, carefully,
and hold it to my chest,
and the tiny mammal will always wriggle away.
My heart sparks and says, 'Do not crush it!
Do not hold it so tightly! You will hurt it!'
The tiny mammal leaps for the floor and disappears.
Why do I dream of such clumsy cruelty,
fed by good intentions and a well-placed heart,
when I could hold out a handful of grass
or vegetables or parsley for vitamin C,
which guinea pigs, like humans,
cannot create on their own?
Why not parley with them,
attend the Tiny Mammal House biannual meeting
and beg forgiveness for my dream-self?
Sit in the old stables at Staglands
for an audience with the buck
bunny-rugging on a bale of hay?
Then, would the guilt I wake up with wriggle away?
Ah, they are just dreams, and I will understand
when I have rabbits of my own

17

not to take shades to heart.
Yes, in the quest for affection,
tiny mammals prefer to approach a still candidate
    rather than be chased.
So, if they do not care for it,
I invite them to run away.

Jardine on Auden, Williams, and Hammond
on Bruegel the Elder

a boy falls from the sky
a man paints an unaffected context for him to fall into
two men write poems concerned with the not-noticing
and another man paints a suggestive dribble
this time with birdfolk in profile
looking beyond the event

so many ways for man to say 'I did not see'

well, I did
and I could have done it better

Gin Sonnet

in memory of the Gibbs' family pool

we threw a playhouse in the pool!   took off
our clothes for extracurricular fun!
this unstoppable December   such luck
each trag kid with a holiday season
birthday in full revolt   and the Bombay
so cold in the mouth   like oil on ice
swimming down to the tiny plastic door
suburban summer   tangle of murmurs
um   I remember the bathtub but not
the bath   just a great pounding in my head
walking the block home wrapped in a sad towel
and the party would have gone unnoticed
if not for the word   CUNNILINGUS   etched
onto the garden path in pale pink chalk

Potholes and K-holes

a hungry dog raided the tent of a prodigal son
busy selling drugs at the other end of the valley

we hacked and laughed and spat out our drinks
and stood back
my sister got bit as a kid because she tried to separate
a dog and a plastic bag

we do not fuck with hunger in a 'sleeps four' tent

witness: the finest shadow puppets this side of the Cobb!
to delight and amaze all eyes at any stage of glaze!
it feels good to be useful
and we are all genuinely impressed
when one member of the party exhibits a bong he made
from a fire extinguisher
with real tenderness

we are gentle folk in a new map
humming
see the way young Harrison Ford lookalike lets
the huhu beetle reorient itself from the perch of his knuckles

the ultraviolet lights are sucking everything in
the pitch-black of the bush is brought out to meet us   help!
I am at home in a bustling laundromat of crickets?

festivals are really about how many legs you have
we share stick-on jewels
and we sweat them all off
we carry water at all times
and keep track of the headcount

someone washed their hands under the septic tank tap
   by accident
and had to respawn at an earlier save point
a secret sacrificed to crack our jaws apart
but back at camp

sunk deep in canvas chairs
eyes shut   bodies bobbing
riding horses in their heads   they say nothing

we leave them be
in their velvet-lined holes
pallid comets throbbing bleakly

Passing Comment from a Man Dressed in White
Wearing Sunglasses Impatiently Pacing the Queue of
Cars Waiting to Board the Interislander Ferry on a
Hot Day in Picton, Delivered through the Window
on the Passenger's Side with All the Grace of an
Unravelling Ham Sandwich

'You wouldn't want to have diarrhoea on a day like this.'

Power Cut at Hotel Coral

Tony is a great name for a cat but today I am
remembering Banana the black Labrador and the
way she watched a sure, handsome man cross
the dancefloor with a piece of bread in his hand for
her and a deft kiss for the nice woman on the couch
next to her (which Banana allows because the bread
is chewy, and the man is nice too). We clicked early
that the owner of the hotel and his head waiter had
the same name (I have forgotten it now) and Tony
was not allowed in the rooms, not that he minded,
the toasted wicker chairs in the dining room
without walls suiting him fine, his floor-to-ceiling
cat tower at reception standing empty and dusty
like a modern Minoan palatial complex – but the
night the band came to play, and she was singing
'perhaps, perhaps, perhaps,' and twenty more Doris
Days sloughed themselves from the chairs and naff
decorative fishing-net hammocks to populate the
tiles and tip their hips out of time, where was Tony?
Banana swung her nose to the sea. The lights went
out and the chorus were sucked mid-strophe into
the blackness of Crete's south coast, still singing
and dancing. The band grew brave and kept playing
without power, the hotel owner leaned in the one lit
window frame and tried to find the fuse box, and
Tony, I can remember now, was interrupting the
glow of the solar lamps at intervals on the edge of
the grass, putting one paw in front of the other in
a slow, spoilt saunter along the low rock wall that
curved around the coast to the next hotel.

Maltesers

for Mum

last week my mum ticked off a whole museum for
displaying a map of the Mediterranean that had a
label for Lampedusa but not Malta, a surprise given
that the latter is a larger landmass by some two
hundred and ninety-six kilometres squared, but it's
not their fault our heritage has been eclipsed by a
sphere of malted milk coated in chocolate – and that
story you told me, which I can never get away from,
of the time when you were a girl, eating Maltesers
in Malta, and you thought they seemed a little
chewy, so you bit one in two, and realised you had
been eating chocolate-coated maggots – it's hard to
get away from feeling like you are the fly, doing the
best you can for your young on a crowded ship

To a Young Pūtakitaki Swimming on the Ōtākaro

young man, tell me where you're going
borne boat-like downstream
if I were to wade in now, to call
and you berthed in my palm
would I find you waxy to the touch?
not timber, not pitch
cool, flat, smooth and faultless
more than could be said
for this river, this city
and this rhythm
duck, I love you

Thoughts Thought After Surveying the Contents of the Fridge

after Ogden Nash's 'Thoughts Thought After A Bridge Party'

My father has several university degrees,
but none of them prepared him
for opening a block of cheese.

I praise the patience and precision he displays in his art,
but he can't open resealable cheese packaging without
    undermining the resealable part.

At home, only he can claim the title of Professor,
but the way he opens a block of cheese
is akin to unwrapping a bar of chocolate
by putting it in the food processor.

My father is right to scorn the hospital café's scone fee,
but if he must work all day and come home hungry,
couldn't he spare one more moment
to consider the long-term goals of the cheese?

When his behaviour is beyond reproach,
    I'm known to call him 'Dad,'
but a block of cheese opened by my father
is not only savaged but dry and daubed with condiments
and not in its rightful place
(a reusable beeswax cheese bag).

My father's appetite dawns upon him severely
    and randomly,
which is why when he has finished lacerating
an easy-peel resealable block of cheese
he gets the scissors and cuts open the cereal
below the ziplock bag line, thus enabling
the equilibrium of the moisture in the pantry.

My father is educated, witty, adept at interpreting
    dinnertime auspices,
but he opens a block of cheese
as delicately as a Labrador retriever
    fondles a tray of sausages.

My Sister (a Cancer) Generously Gives Her Dog to
Our Parents
for my family

my sister has a nice name
doesn't mean I like it when my mum looks me in the eyes
and uses it on me

years later my boss tells me that the best way
to get a dog's attention
is to call the other dog's name
provided you have two dogs
the trick always works
and so on with sisters
I am jealous of her
star sign
she is the crab and I am the tampon
but I am understanding

understanding and graceful
the young Libra sun and moon that I am
I work hard to make sure they get our names right
at school where hers is in gold on the good walls
and my brother, a Capricorn
plays timpani in the orchestra to make a statement

when I was little
I ransacked my sister's sticker collection
and made a collage of her blue-chip playground stocks

on the legs of her full-sized single bed
which I was so envious of

she didn't hold it against me

when I was bigger
I read her journal
itemised all the things she hid
   under her enormous double bed
ratted her out for having Smirnoff Double Blacks
   in her t-shirt drawer

she didn't hold that against me either

but
the thing
that makes my sister purse her lips
is that I have never adopted a pet
and then left the country
and now Frank has made a serious error
(but good luck explaining that to him)

he has stolen my mother's best breast
and run off down the garden

Oarfish

'The most beautiful fish ever obtained on the coasts
of New Zealand'
— Julius von Haast

harbinger of doom, O oarfish
with flesh so gelatinous!
are we all about to be squished,
harbinger of doom, O oarfish?
down where the sea and crust kiss,
do you forewarn continental flatulence?
harbinger of doom, O oarfish
with flesh so gelatinous!

Field Notes on Elegy

a downside to being a fairly competent singer
is that no one has ever serenaded me

and how I love poor singers!
no matter how toneless
I am your best friend at karaoke, yet

it is one thing to sing along with something on the radio
or follow the creep of colour
and language in the foreground
of a stranger's holiday in Rome or Nepal
and quite another
to stand still
lungs full of breath
swallowing one's heart

        when we were seated at the dinner
            I said I was leaving
          no one got to their feet

           I try not to think the ancient thoughts
    but in my head there was always something
                ancient about this
            as if years ago our ancestors met
                  at a dusty table
                    and agreed

I was writing myself into scenes that were not happening
casting my eyes across rooms we were not in
standing   jilted
in the doorway or on the stairs
of a dark and over-furnished country house
in an empire. silhouette. dress.
just to enhance the embarrassment of feeling

O 'haunted wheelbarrow'
O, 'walking over glass // to reach the other man'

I am a hopeless Roman
writhing on a chaise longue
legs supported
wits adrift

or the Lady of Shalott
catching sight of my cracked reflection across the room
all for Lancelot and his 'tirra lirra'
my weaving ruined

. . . sī nōstri ōblītă tăcērĕt
sāna ēssēt. nŭnc quōd gānnĭt ĕt ōblŏquĭtŭr
nōn sōlūm mĕmĭnīt sĕd quaē mūlto ācrĭŏr ēst rēs
īrātā est. hŏc ēst ūrĭtŭr ĕt lŏquĭtŭr.

if she were silent, so forgetful of us,
she could be sane – now! she grumbles and interrupts!

because not only does she remember, but,
what is more dazzling, she is furious.
that's it – she burns and she speaks.

I walk amid the altars until my name feels like a dactyl again
play the spaniel under the table at the great feast
place my big heavy head in the laps of family and friends

feed sacred chickens and hope for good news

[[Catullus was a whinger who put too much trust in being
read, but if one was to ask Sulpicia, Sempronia, Clodia,
Sappho, what do you think they would say??]]

when we do meet
I lose my mind for a minute
briefly consider painting my name on a little boat
and staging my own death
float downriver just to hear you call me
fair

patience   and ferocity
        what would my namesake think?
    kept awake at night by so many lyres being restrung
        hoping for the sound of footsteps in the garden
so   Propertian

34

and if sincerity frightens you
tough luck
I am below your window
chewing on my tender thoughts
like Atthis in her fragment, shining
and conspicuous

you don't have to look
you don't have to listen
but the karaoke machine will get here soon and
that might make things difficult

Mad Dog

Palatine Anthology V.266 — Paulus Silentiarius

they say a man attacked by a mad dog
sees a phantom of the beast
in every body of water

did rabid Love fix its keen teeth in me
and maraud my soul with mania?

for you – [ggrRRR]   you – [rrrrRUF]   you – [rrrRA]
you – [ggRArArA]   your – [ghhHAhHAhHAh]

your delightful image appears in my whirlpools and rivers
my open sea
my glass of wine

Puttanesca

I have come to this flat where your friends are
hanging out to sit and let the good wine I absorbed
at the Classics Department's Christmas party burn
off. One guest reports that he is 'sick of how shocked
everyone acts about stuff,' and his example is the
Holocaust. He lines his hole well for the winter,
complains piteously about the tendency of others to
be 'triggered' by such discussions. Your shirt buttons
are set to summer, a Star of David is hanging flat
between your collarbones. Neither of us know why
this man is here, but you feed him anyway. Our host
is so drunk, he tries to balance his plate on the arm
of the sofa. The plate tips and a large portion of
puttanesca slides straight into his lap. Our host is so
drunk he cannot act shocked. His girlfriend scoops up
the food with her hands and slaps it back on the plate.
No one worries about the stains. It is not that sort
of place. I am thrilled that you are offering to walk
me home, and as we move, I watch for auspices. Two
snails climb a wall. Some wingshape passes overhead.
A stranger approaches with a bleeding leg. You leave
me at my door. Each step, hallway and window frame
feels like a tiny bereavement.

While Cooking Kūmara and Onion Fritters

drop heaped spoonfuls into the pan and
burn because I am not used to my parents' induction
    stovetop and
it would be a lie to describe their fry-pan as 'non-stick' and
you are asking me if I am 'alright?' and
I have to explain why I am home early for the holidays
    and alone and
not think too long about the way you say 'interesting'
    twice and
'interesting' and
practical and accustomed to German kitchen technology
    you lower the heat and
set the table for four and
fairly apportion the burnt offerings and
dissipate this long evening's fluster

I am ready to carve the pomegranate now
I am ready to play Scrabble
I am ready to lose

Stone Fruit

they tumble down the bank at two different speeds
yet still in duet, comically flushed and buxom
against the backdrop of waifs playing heroines
written by a playwright who was definitely more
of an ass man, a poet could be more specific,
remembering something someone said in a writing
class about 'geraniums' not 'flowers' etcetera but
I forget to note the genus of the fruit because you
are swinging a leg from nowhere to intercept them
like a goblin shark revealing the true extent of its
protrusible upper jaw oh this is why I made myself
late, I am thinking about asking if you would like
to go swimming

The Perch

Palatine Anthology V.268 — Paulus Silentiarius

fear no more the swift lead of longing
fuckin' Love has emptied its quiver in me

shiver not at the approach of wings
the acrid talons of Love have me
pinned

I am the perch on which Love preens
unruffled, just sitting, no thoughts of change

Raspberries

in two hours and fourteen lines of Horace
there's going to be a confession

I pass the time like any free woman would
lodge a false claim to being shaky on the vocab

research the difference between Proteus
    and Proetus
because we are going to do this properly, alright?
of course readers will know the difference

things have not been the same inside my brain
since I watched you examine that bicycle tube earlier

running that sticky black snake through your hands
I wondered if you noticed

plucking the aphids from the bowl of raspberries
I wondered if you noticed

someone spilt freshly ground coffee
    all over the bench this morning
it was me

fumbling in the mess of my progenitors' kitchen
single-origin bashfulness

must haul my voice from the rush of blushing
must say something now so I can sleep

there is a reason our writing club didn't make it
you were the hardest friend I ever kept

Stay Cruel

a translation of Horace's Ode 3.7

why are you crying   Asterie   for your steady
faithful young man   whom the sweet westerly winds
which blow at the beginning of Spring will return to you
rich   from his work in Thynus   why are you crying
for Gyges   Asterie?

though driven by mean southerlies to Oricos
stuck following the senseless constellation of Capricorn
your Gyges gets through the night   just a little
very   sleepless and sad
  but

Chloe   his hostess   is getting excited
and her emissaries try with a thousand subtleties
'oh!'   they say   'Chloe is sighing   burned!
by the fire Gyges holds for Asterie!'   they say
'there once was a faithless woman!!   and!!
she impelled her gullible Proetus with some   !!false!!
accusations to kill Bellerophon   so pure!
well before his time   and and and'
they say
  'did you hear about how Peleus
was almost given his idea of Hell
when he fled from Hippolyta of Magnesia
resisting her?'
and so, so specious   they repeat
the stories which teach how to shoot your own feet

in vain   deafer than the rocks of Ikaria
Gyges hears their voices and notices   nothing

but beware   Asterie
lest Enipeus, so   nearby
please you more than would be right

sure   no one rides like he does
across the grass of Mars   so talented . . .

and no one swims like he does
down the veins of the Tiber . . .

as soon as night falls   shut your doors
and don't let his singing   his queries
pull your eyes to the street below
though he keeps calling you
so   disruptive . . .

stay cruel

Pirate

Palatine Anthology V.309 — Diophanes of Myrina

really and truly
Love may be labelled a pirate three times!

pirate!
keeping watch!

pirate!
acting bold!

pirate!
stealing clothes!

Taking the Auspices After a Miscommunication

one karoro atop each lamppost on our street

a thatch of eels all straining
    for the same piece of minced meat

phrases in the wine list: 'grapes with a history
shrouded in mystery'
and 'indigenous yeasts'

a friend of a friend received an abundance of bliss balls
because their house burned down
and they are vegan and coeliac
and people wanted to do something nice for them

I overhear an apostle misuse a demonstrative pronoun
('I love THIS outdoors')
and thus am forced to wonder what other outdoors there are

they are building a hydroslide a few blocks over

after watching *Titanic*, Lily turned to me and said:
'I wonder how many pianos there are in the ocean'

on New Regent Street, a rat king of bicycles

on Moorhouse Ave, a heading dog in the tray of a ute
barking all the way through the traffic

I think we are going to be okay

Encryption Limerick

If a stranger were to gain access
to our exchanges of titillating praxis
surely they'd be engorged
in brain, sheath or sword –
we could invoice for erotodidaxis!

Tramping Fragment #2

pūtakitaki bleat in duet along a bright valley
and [with beech branches] the shade
is shadowed and down from wasp homes
[   ] worry comes

a horse blooms like spring
like an anxious classicist
    [   ]

not one girl I think
who looks on [you smoking in her mother's jacket]
       will ever
       have [hubbub
       like] this

Raisinhood

Palatine Anthology V.304 — Anonymous

unripe, you refused me

fresh and ready, you passed me by

even so

grant me a little of your raisinhood

Adoration of the Magi, Ōtākaro

a camel, an ass, an ox and I look upon you with awe

there is no collective noun for a group of octopuses
because they are solitary creatures
making fried egg dinners for one
taking weeks to get through a box of cereal
feeling guilty for owning
   more than two open packets
   of pasta at once
but imagine a collective noun of octopuses
simultaneously losing their grip
I look upon you
dumb fish go free
clouds of shells explode on underwater beaches
so many liquid rocks appear in the sea

it is the right of a camel to have oval blood cells
and drink 200 litres in three minutes
it is the right of an ass to chew hay and be tough
of oxen to low
of three men to be greatly impressed by a baby
and it is your right to find a hold on my life

every smiling dog that jogged past the library
   read the paper this morning
and noted the headline, 'IT IS LOVE:
REDZONE BLACKBIRDS REPORT
ON BAD NIGHT FOR LOCAL WORMS'

in a ghost suburb something has grown
as simple as hands, as clear as pylons

bless the ratepayers and the linemen
they have fashioned a halo for you
here at last on a crumbling footpath
comes the familiarity of something new

discipule, quickener
longblacksplashofcoldmilkonesugar
in the focus of this somewhere I will miss
the staggering days of not knowing what to do with my face
when you are holding it

I look upon you
and giddiness toddles out of the bathroom in the hall
and the hanging pictures collect a shoulder charge each
you need only speak to bring the fifteenth century back
we will gather round and build the bravura
I know a guy with a cow

Some Auxiliary Findings of Falling in Love with a Member of the Green Party

my feelings for you are like double cab utes
    in an urban environment
once I recognised their size
and their inconvenience to all other road users
they were everywhere

the way I feel about you is the afternoon
with a temperature of twenty-seven degrees in late May
something scientists
and our mutual friend who has a diploma
    in environmental management
predicted years ago

my feelings for you are like discovering
in the time it takes to charge the battery
    of a Nissan Leaf to seven percent
you can get to second base on its back seat

this way I feel about you
is nothing like the percentage of utes
observed in an Auckland University city traffic survey
that were actually using their tray to carry something:

nine˙percent

Notes

The Lord Byron quote in 'Ode to Mons Pubis' comes from the poem 'Childe Harold's Pilgrimage', published between 1812 and 1818.

'Rural Activities' is about a grand day out in Sheffield.

'Is It Hard to Follow Your Heart When You Have Three?' is a sad story, really. I suggest you do not look up what happened to the octopus. Just leave your imagination here, in this poem. Claudius Aelianus (c. 175–235 CE), commonly known as Aelian, wrote *On The Nature of Animals* (*De Natura Animalium*) by drawing on earlier written accounts of natural history which are now lost. His work is valuable and at times eccentric.

'When We Were Courting' is inspired by a fabulous Antonio Canova statue titled 'Theseus and the Minotaur', made in Rome in 1782 and currently on display in the Victoria and Albert Museum in London.

'My Iron Cervix' takes its title from the 1994 Radiohead song 'My Iron Lung'.

'Disturbing Suburban Magic Trick' was written about Cilla, our family dog (an excitable Huntaway, d. 2020), and Lieutenant Leonard Handford Jardine (1890–1969), my great-granduncle.

'Tiny Mammal Dream' is inspired by a 1967 poem by Fleur Adcock titled 'The Pangolin'.

'Jardine on Auden, Williams, and Hammond on Bruegel the Elder' refers to the following items: the poem 'Musée des Beaux Arts' by W. H. Auden, the poem 'Landscape with the Fall of Icarus' by William Carlos Williams, the 1995 painting *The Fall of Icarus (after Bruegel)* by Bill Hammond, and the c. 1560 painting *Landscape with the Fall of Icarus* by Pieter Bruegel the Elder.

'Gin Sonnet' is for my friends from high school, in memory of supporting each other through the earthquake years. My thanks to the Gibbs family for the use of their swimming pool.

'Potholes and K-holes' is inspired by an influential visit to the Twisted Frequency festival.

'Passing Comment . . .' is a true story.

'Thoughts Thought After Surveying the Contents of the Fridge' takes its title from, and is inspired by, a 1949 poem by Ogden Nash titled 'Thoughts Thought After A Bridge Party'.

'Oarfish' is a triolet inspired by that most miraculous and interesting fish, *Regalecus glesne*.

'Field Notes on Elegy' contains several lines of Catullus 83, both in scanned Latin and in English translated by me. The poem also quotes 'Monica' by Hera Lindsay Bird, 'Sabina, and the Chain of Friendship' by Anna Jackson, 'The Lady of Shalott' by Lord Alfred Tennyson and Sappho fragment 96. Sulpicia and Sappho were two of the foremost poets of antiquity. Sempronia features in Sallust's *Bellum Catilinae*. Clodia is widely believed to be the real name of one of the elegiac subjects of Catullus's poetry.

'Stay Cruel' was translated for, and first performed at, a special event in the 2021 Toi Art public programme at The Museum of New Zealand Te Papa Tongarewa. I was invited by Chris Tse to respond to the 1904 painting *Asterié* by Sir Edward Poynter, the subject of which is the character Asterie from Horace's 'Ode 3.7'.

'Taking the Auspices After a Miscommunication' is inspired by the ancient Roman religious practice of augury. An augur would observe and interpret the behaviour of birds and, depending on the birds' behaviour, would decide whether the signs were auspicious (favourable) or inauspicious (unfavourable). I have extended the practice to include observations beyond whatever important things birds might be doing.

'Tramping Fragment #2' is inspired by the poetic fragments of Sappho.

'Some Auxiliary Findings of Falling in Love with a Member of the Green Party' includes statistics from Toby Morris's 30 June 2021 webcomic 'The Side Eye's Two New Zealands: The Double Cab Climate' published on *The Spinoff*.

My thanks to the editors and publishers of the following publications in which some of these poems first appeared: *Capital Magazine*, *The Friday Poem*, *Landfall*, *The Map*, *Mayhem*, *Mimicry*, *New Zealand Poetry Shelf*, *Poetry Aotearoa Yearbook 2023*, *The Spinoff*, *Sport*, *Starling*, *Stasis*, *takahē* and *Turbine / Kapohau*.

Bibliography

Bird, Hera Lindsay, *Hera Lindsay Bird*, Victoria University Press, 2017.

Jackson, Anna, *Pasture and Flock: New & Selected Poems*, Auckland University Press, 2018.

Paton, W. R., *The Greek Anthology*, Harvard University Press, Cambridge, MA, 1916.

Acknowledgements

I get to do that thing now. This is my book! This is my time to acknowledge people! And there are so many of you! Strap in.

I was fortunate to be tutored by many great writers, and I want them all to know that their interest in what I was up to and their suggestions about how to proceed helped me a great deal. My thanks to Tusiata Avia and Grace Taylor for running those spoken word workshops way back in 2012 that got me thinking about poetry in performance. Thank you to Margaux Hlavac, Daisy Lavea-Timo, Michelle McDonald and the rest of the English and Creative & Performing Arts teachers from my time at Cashmere High School. My special thanks to Denise Winskill, who is no longer with us, and who I think of every time I read Seamus Heaney.

Thank you to Hinemoana Baker for your knowledge and guidance, your paper at the IIML pushed me and I loved it. Thank you to Harry Ricketts for always making time for a coffee and a chat about poetry or novels or television or music or whatever magpie-thing you have ready! Thank you to Anna Jackson for always taking my poems on their own scrappy terms and finding such lovely things to say about them (and thanks for feeding me, on several occasions). My humble thanks to the School of Languages and Cultures at VUW for supporting me as a student and to the staff for teaching me several ancient languages. Julia Simons, Mark Masterson, Simon Perris, Diana Burton, Jeff Tatum, Judy

Deuling, James Kierstead, Babette Puetz – thanks
for being great language teachers! I could not have
written *BITER* without you.

I really need to make a song and dance about how
grateful I am for the existence of *Starling* magazine
and its editors, Francis Cooke and Louise Wallace.
Starling introduced me to so many talented people,
and now some of them are my very good friends and
I think that's neat. So, to the late night karaoke crowd
at TK BBQ and the press of people in Book Hound
on Riddiford Street, I say I am glad to know you and
thank you! So much! Thanks Francis, Louise, Chris,
Rebecca, Rebecca, Ruby, Sinead, Freya, Eleanor, Tayi,
Emma, Ash, Stacey, essa, Rose, Jordan and Joy.

My thanks to Rhys Feeney and Ria Masae for
being my page buddies in *AUP New Poets 7*. I am
grateful that we had the opportunity to come into
the world of publishing together. Thank you to the
AUP team for looking after us.

Thank you to Te Matatiki Toi Ora The Arts
Centre (especially Chris, Terri, Hannah and Liz),
the Teece Museum of Classical Antiquities, Creative
New Zealand and The Stout Trust for the wonderful
residency in 2021. The Arts Four Creative Residency
programme was a massive learning curve for me,
and several of these poems were written under your
shelter. Jo Burzynska, Ana Iti and Julie Hill, y'all
were fantastic co-residents and taught me a lot. More
than words and wigs could express! You must know
that I think fondly of the time we spent together!
My thanks also to Claire Mabey and the Verb Readers
& Writers Festival team for all the work you have
been doing over the last eight years, for the micro

residency during Verb 2021, and for letting me share
that residency with Nathan Joe and Ataria Sharman
who were also fantastic co-residents.

To my parents, David and Ruth. This is the book
I was telling you about. Thanks for supporting me
throughout my studies, reading to me and taking me
all over the world. To my siblings, Maddie and Max.
You have always made me feel like a rockstar even when
I was actually super cringe. To Gran Jan, I think you're
really cool and I am so glad to have you in my life.
Thank you for all of the books! To my family, Jardines,
Waterworths, Andrews and Attards. You help me know
who I am and what my voice sounds like. I am not sure
what Grandma Rose and Grandpa Derek would have
made of these poems, or Jim for that matter. Let's hope
that somewhere they're laughing.

I would like to mihi to the mana whenua of Aotearoa.
I thank you for the generosity you have shown to five
generations of my Pākehā whānau, a generosity which
has allowed me to thrive here despite the disrespect
shown to you by us, your Treaty partners. I am grateful
to be here, and I am grateful that my mother, a more
recent arrival, has been made welcome here too.

To my friends!!! Audrey Banach-Salas, Ziming Liu,
Rebecca Hawkes, Peter Scriven, Will Moot, Will Searle,
Jack & Steph van Beynen, Eilish Draper, Matthew
Martel, Steven Thomas, George Fenn, Philip Jones,
John Gibbs, Poppia Marriott, McKenzie Dowson,
Emma Shi, Klarysse Berquist, Harry & Belinda, Simon
& Jen, my flatmates, my neighbours in Addington –
let's party!

My thanks to the early readers and champions of
BITER. Josiah Morgan, Kerry Donovan, Francis Cooke,

Erik Kennedy, Ziming Liu, Rebecca Hawkes, Vana Manasiadis, Harry Ricketts and Anna Jackson – I think you're all wonderful and I am grateful for your time and your brains.

BITER began as a zine I made for my boyfriend. Henceforth all who enjoy it should forward their thanks to Nathaniel Herz-Edinger, the earliest reader of these poems. Let this book serve as a warning for any who would go around whispering lines of Catullus in Latin, in metre, into an unsuspecting ear before abruptly vanishing into the night.

Author photo: Petra Mingneau

Claudia Jardine has an MA in classics with
distinction from Victoria University of Wellington,
where she won the 2020 Alex Scobie Research Prize
and a Marsden Grant for Masters scholarship.
Her first chapbook, 'The Temple of Your Girl', was
published in *AUP New Poets 7*. Her ancestors are from
the British Isles and the Maltese Archipelago, and she
lives in Ōtautahi. There are lots of wonderful things
about living in Ōtautahi – for example, have you
ever seen the royal spoonbill, or kōtuku ngutupapa,
feeding in the estuary at dusk? Marvellous.